Like a

Sunflower

A COLLECTION
OF POETRY
AND PROSE

Made in Australia

ISBN: 978-0-9756101-0-7

Written by KEXA
Edited by my husband, Ken
Illustrations and Designs by Niokoba

In the midst of the darkest days,
I wish to be like a sunflower.
It never stops *searching for light*
even in its most *difficult moments.*

Just as it stands unwavering,
weathering the storms that come its way
I, too, will have
better and *sunshiny days.*

With determination,
I will endeavour to *keep going,*
embracing the hopeful light
that awaits beyond the shadows.

Excerpt from
Like a Sunflower

to my *family*
who instilled in me
the value of hard work
and perseverance

to all my *friends* in Midland
who supported and encouraged me
on my creative journey

to my greatest supporter
my *husband*, KEN
I can, because of you

and to *you*.
this book is affectionately dedicated.

Prologue

As I travel along words and verses,
my soul embarks on a heartfelt journey
through the life's many emotions and
experiences. Within these pages, you'll
discover a collection of thoughts,
each carefully woven with strings of joy,
sorrow, hope, and despair –
reflections of moments that have touched
my heart, a mirror to my innermost feelings,
and a portrait of my soul's expression.

This book extends an invitation,
a hand to hold, as we enter a world
where words transcend into emotions
and lines unfold into stories.
Every whisper from my heart to yours,
bridging a heartfelt connection between
you and me.

As you leaf through the pages,
I invite you to open not only your eyes
but your heart and mind,
that may you find solace and inspiration
as we share this beautiful journey,
your path intertwining with mine.

Table of Contents

I

Searching For Light

Her

Her reality
has always been
a series of stops and starts.

She's there,
blending into the dusk,
but still trying to glimmer
like a star.

Often labelled as cruel
for mastering the art of boundaries,
for having a cold heart.
In her most muted hues and shades,
she still creates her own art.

In the ebbs and flows of her journey,
challenges cascade upon her
like sheets of black and white.
Yet, she stands unafraid,
having conquered the darkest of nights.

She's trying,
growing, and doing
whatever she can to thrive.

She's a poem
too powerful to read,
the one she never got
the chance to write.

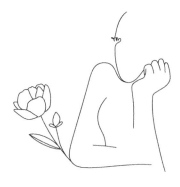

Becoming

A ton of baggage to pack and carry,
emotions I never knew I needed
until I learned what they meant to me.
With me are my worries and unknown fears,
missed chances and few condensed thrills.

I realised -
I've lost a lot of opportunities
by letting my terrors weigh me down.
Missed again the opportunity,
To let these trials embolden me.

Yet slowly –
Slowly, I will let them go.
Slowly, I will set them free.
I will not be stopped.
I will not be held captive by fear.
Just as I did when I was young and carefree,
I'll fall in love with life once again.

I am moving along.

I am becoming more.

This Year

Looking back –
How quickly time has passed, and I have hardly
noticed this year go by. I've realised that my life
for these past few months were as if a book
with chapters of highs and lows.
I know not what's been written on the next page
as I feel like an empty space on some days
and a thoughtless draft on some nights.

But then –
As I write my story, I've come to understand that
mistakes are an unavoidable part of the journey,
but that doesn't mean they can't be valuable lessons.
Despite the chaos all around me, this year has
taught me to embrace the uncertainties of life
and all that it entails.

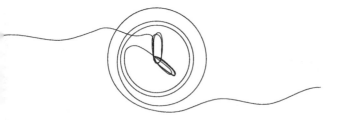

I have learned how to cut down every rope that's
tied me down and has stopped me from living in
the moment. I have learned to take as much time as
necessary to experience different realities and allow
myself the opportunity to understand –
regardless of its permanence or not.

I am here –
Relishing every chance that knocks on my door and
forgiving myself for taking too long to accept defeat
and failure. Maybe this year isn't the best by any
means, but somehow, it's reflective. It's through this
that I am craving for more experiences, more telling
days, more chances, and do-overs.

Here's to a life with whatever unfolds
to a life I want to manifest
to a life which is both –
my adventure and respite.

Good Things in Disguise

Maybe this time,
after all I've been through,
I can tell there is always
something wonderful that comes
from every bad experience.

Whenever I relive
every failure and rejection,
it makes me understand more
why things happen the way they do.

It's not enjoyable in the least
but I believe life steered and re-directed me
to the path should really be on.

I may still be far
from my intended destination,
but every detour and roadblock
have made me better,
braver, and wiser.

This journey is not a walk in the park
but even flowers need a little rain to bloom,
and even in a heavy downpour, the sun still
shines, and I know one day –

So will I.

You and Me, Both

On days like this
I know I leave myself out
so much.

On days like this
I have to remind myself
that it's alright to feel upset and sad,
that it's alright to break down and cry.

On days like this
I have to remember that it's alright
to feel pain whenever things
are too heavy to bear and too hard to accept.

Everyone goes through hard times,
I know this phase will end –
so a new one can begin.

If you and I are on the same boat,
let's not lose our sight on chasing the sunset.
When life gives us choppy waters,
let's roll with the tide and continue surfing
the waves.

It will be a challenging ride, but as long as
there are stars in the sky, we get unlimited wishes
and chances for a life as promising as
a beautiful sunrise every morning.

Let's not give up on life for having bad days.
Like they always say, it's just a bad day,
not a bad life. This, too, shall pass,
and little by little, we'll be okay.

You and me, both.

Waiting

I take comfort in knowing that –
what comes easy does not last
and the things that last,
do not come easy.

Great things don't happen overnight.
Like seeds that need nurturing
to grow and blossom,
they require time, patience, and sacrifice.

I may be a way's away
but when I'm finally there,
It will all be clear to me –

the wait is always necessary.

New Beginnings

What feels like waiting pointlessly
could be life's way of preparing
something more significant
than I could comprehend.

More often than not,
things have to come to an end
and be forgotten
for better things to begin.

Tiny Victories

It is a complex world I live in.
There are so many restricting walls,
barriers that push me back,
a lot of fences to climb,
and they are continually getting
higher and higher.

Some places seem unreachable,
directions are ambiguous and unclear,
and unfriendly characters
defying me along the way.

Yet I'll never be frightened to take chances,
especially if it means turning my life around.
I'll never remain rooted in the same spot
because progress must not be constrained.
I'll never be afraid to allow myself to grow
and pursue what I believe is best for me.

Even though not every endeavour
is a promised success, all the learnings
from every failure and downfall
are invaluable tiny victories in itself.

Little Steps

Extraordinary things are done
by a series of small steps
brought together.
So here I am,
taking it from
one thing to another,
one step at a time.

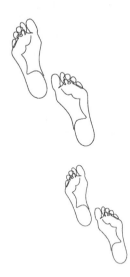

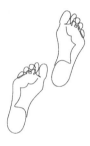

And just like me,
 you may be nowhere near
  where you want to be,
   you may be still on a different road
    or probably stranded on
     the curbside of success
      but as long as you can walk,
       even on barefoot,
        you and I will find our way
         and we will eventually get there.

Girl in the Mirror

When I look in the mirror,
I want to clearly see
the battle scars I've healed.

I want to accept the flaws
that have been sewn onto my skin.
I want to see perfection
in the mismatched pieces of myself.

When I look in the mirror,
I want to get back in touch
with who I really am.
I want to give value in what
the rest of the world does not.

I want to respect the parts
of my history that I hate
and be gracious with them.

Even though imperfections
may have been crammed
into this one frail body,
I have faith that one day,
I will be able to accept everything and
express a sheen of tenderness to myself.

My body is my precious sanctuary.
I am now learning to adore it –
the way it should be.

Hard Dreams

The world said
my dreams were too big
But, these dreams were all I had

There were blank pages
I was meant to fill in
There were musings in my head
I was meant to write drown
I wanted to follow where
my aspirations led me
and not pay heed to what others said

I wondered where it would lead me
I leapt, I soared to different heights
thinking there were as many answers
as there were stars in the sky

No matter how daunting
are those that lie ahead,
I have to keep believing
in the roads I have chosen.
I have to have faith that
I can find the star I am seeking.

If I stay on this path,
I should be able to figure out
what matters most to me.

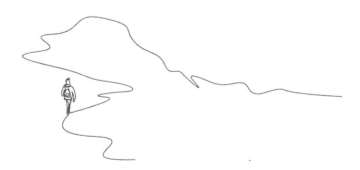

The Love You Deserve

May you find someone who would –

heal you,
understand you,
choose to love you for better and worse.

You may not find a love that is perfect,
but you will find a love that is real.

The kind of love where –
your happiness makes up so much of theirs
because you deserve it.

Living the Life

The world will remember me
for my innocence –
the way I see goodness
in everything.

I want to live a life
where I don't have
to dress with pretensions.

I desire an honest, uninvolved,
and carefree way of living.
I fancy days that are smooth,
spontaneous, and candid.

I prefer to have meaning
and sincerity to my history.
I want a future filled with beauty,
devoid of complexity.

I enjoy curating a life
that allows me to be creative,
clumsy, muddled, and unapologetic
for who I really am.

I want to keep living life
and not just merely exist.
I want to thrive, grow,
and make a difference.

I want to really know
what it means to live.
Knowing myself,
chasing my dreams
and getting through –
day by day.

II

Difficult Moments

Hurling

We must accept that no matter what we do,
there are certain things around us that we cannot control.
Sometimes, we must remind ourselves -
it is how life goes.
We don't have power over other people's thoughts
or their feelings –
and that's okay.

It is ironic that, sometimes, the very thing hurting us
is the same thing that could heal us.
There are a million things that are beyond our control,
and healing only comes when –
we learn to accept what cannot be
and what can be.

Your sense of peace will come when you know how to let go
of what is breaking your heart and trusting that,
in due time –
you're going to be alright.

Easier

Maybe this is why
most people choose to appear strong
to hide pain and suffering.

Playing pretend is easier
than explaining why you're hurting.

Losing

The thing is –

there's no easy way to let go of something
you've grown so used to having around.

The space
The place
The emotions
The memories —

they are irreplaceable.

But sometimes,
we must learn how to move on
from the things that are
unconsciously breaking us.
It takes bravery to decide
when to let them go
or know if they're worth fighting for.

People come and go.
Not all promises are kept.
Hearts are broken and seldom mended.

Some things you may perceive important
but if they no longer serving you well,
they won't help you grow.

Whether things happen for you
or against you,
you should know that –
not everything that weighs you down,
are meant to be burdens.

Sometimes,
you come out strong and victorious.
But remember,
it takes an even stronger person
to admit a loss.

Life Goes On

I will always live by this truth.

Despite the pain,
I somehow manage to get through
disappointments and frustrations
in silence.

Often the grief is unbearable
and my demons come to haunt me,
somehow,
I show up everyday as if I'm not hurting
I still live as if I'm not afraid.

I often choose to conceal what I feel
in fear of others' prejudice.
I hide those that may be used against me.
I hide the tears and make it look like
I am doing okay, and I am happy.

I act strong until being strong
is all I know and all I ever will be.

It is a tough pill to swallow
but I know
no matter how hard I fight my battles,
no matter how much I sacrifice,
whether or not I give my all –

the world will just continue to revolve,

and life will go on,

like it always has,

with or without me.

Broken Dreams

I watched some of my dreams
go down the drain.
I often wondered why
I never got the longings of my heart.

In pursuing them,
I was unable to overcome difficulty.
Yet it's a story worth sharing,
an experience that shaped me.

Some memories came paired with agony,
but from each painful description
I learned to play with words so well
that I managed to make the amazing.

My dreams have always been the most
beautiful parts of me, and now,
they've all come crashing down.
But I will always remember them.

Maybe some dreams
are not there to be realised.

Maybe these broken dreams
are meant to lead me elsewhere.

Some Time Alone

I have always been
vulnerable and defenceless.
Sometimes I feel as if
I am not strong enough to handle challenges
and I get pushed to the edge.

In moments in which I feel
optimistic, hopeful, driven, and capable,
I have also seen versions of myself
that wants to hide away and shy myself
from the rest of the world.

For a time,
I desired to become just another
forgotten memory.
I wanted to cower in a quiet little corner
and bask in obscurity.

I have wanted to be lost and not be found.

Unconditional

I pray –

you find a person
who will never judge you,
no matter your circumstances
or how contradicting
and unpredictable you are,
how aimless your arguments are,
or how challenging it is to love you
during your darkest moments.

Regardless of how long
the search may last,
how unclear the path may be,
or how many broken hearts
are scattered along the way,
may you always have faith in love.

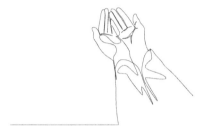

I pray –

you get the kind of love that will help you
mend your heart as you heal
from the wounds you don't show the world.

Art of Letting Go

I grasped an idea of you
as I try to untangle my thoughts,
feeling that forever is not destined for us.

No matter what we do
despite our best efforts,
fate insists we drift apart.

In the lifetimes beyond,
if chance reared its head
there might be you and I.

In another life,
with destiny on our side
we just might be together.

If it were a different reality,
without any of our history,
there lies a strong you and me.

Next Time

My journey to love
may lead me somewhere else
possibly to places where you'll also be

But one thing is for certain
it is going to find its way
a way, where, it gets
all the love it deserves –

when it comes next time.

Temporary

Even after all this time,
you still have a special place in my heart.
Despite the chaos on the countertops,
the lies hidden inside empty cups
your name is still etched in my mind.

You were my most intense heartache,
yet I feel a stream of bliss whenever
I ponder on the things we almost had.

> *At the very least,*
> *I knew what it was like to be in love.*

Despite the hurtful reality that
we didn't get a happy ending,
we shared beautiful moments of happiness
we could dearly treasure.

> *Even though fleeting,*
> *I don't regret loving you at all.*

Albeit temporary –
it was beautiful while it lasted.

What It Takes

It takes bravery –

to hold on to a single reason
when life is throwing
a thousand reasons at you
to give up.

It takes bravery –

to move forward and walk with hope,
even if your days have been filled with
heavy downpours.

It takes bravery –

to bet on yourself even
when it feels like the world
has turned its back on you.

It takes bravery –

to mend yourself when you're in tatters,
with many missing pieces, mismatched patterns,
and hues faded by enfeebled emotion.

And it takes bravery –

to remain of strong mind
while waiting for the right time
to heal and blossom again.

Alone Again

Sometimes it's not the unspoken words
that haunt me but from them -
the possible responses that I fear.

I feel as if it's better to be tormented
by the different what-ifs
than to grieve over memories I've shared with another.

I will always choose
to make peace with my lack of courage
rather than regretting taking a risk.

It feels better knowing I let people go,
instead of dragging them
into my pit of misery.

At times I believe that people are safer without me,
and I find a deeper sense of peace
when I'm alone.

I am too tired to let everyone know -
I had already gone once the sun was up.

Chances

This just might be
the universe's way of saving me.
Saving me from a pain that hurts so bad
that it ushered me to a different road
to rebuilding myself again.

You still might think I'm here for you.
You might think my heart
can be tempted at any time
but here for you, I am no longer.

I've now learned to keep myself
safe at a distance.
Even though I have shunned our past,
I could not escape the grief
my heart felt from being with you.

Our beautiful memories still linger.
And if ever we meet again,
I hope the universe
will play its part once more.

We'll either want to try again
or agree unequivocally
that we're not meant to be.

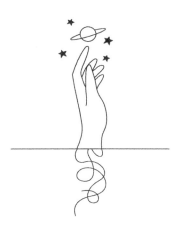

The Old Days

Gone are the times
  when everything moved so slowly.

   Times when my plights
    were handed over to the moon
    Times where bright stars
    were my only companions
    Times when only scars
    knew the touch of my skin

     Gone are the days
      when my fears would always win.

Gone are the days
  of unrealistic reveries.

    All the bridges I hardly crossed
     and sunsets I mindlessly chased
      All the melancholic rhythms
       and muddled schemes
        All these unaligned memories
         put my heart in a drunken daze

     It's all gone.

Moving On

It used to terrify me –
The long process of healing,
hurting with no end in sight,
afraid of losing my best years,
wallowing in my misery.

It would consume my nights
with tears I couldn't control
and drown me in an ocean of regret.
I spent dreading the months that come
would be an echoing sound reminding me
of how I hate myself

for not being enough
for not giving my all
for not being the best one

But then, as I walked out of your life,
I realised how constrained that place was.
I realised how - you and I -
deluded me into thinking that it was
the only place that would welcome me.

And now that you've left me,
I tried to rediscover the world
I used to roam before you.

This new reality made me realise
there's so much more beauty and love here
than what we could have ever shared.

There's so much more out there
than pleading for you to stay
when you no longer want to.

Just Another Heartbreak

There's nothing I have left to sacrifice.

I deliberately let my world revolve around
you, when, at the end of it all –
You were just drifting with the tide
You were just another person
I was meant to pass and sail by.

I could have loved you the best way
I could possibly ever love someone.
But like how broken bones mend,
I let my heart break –

> *'til it became a better version*
> *of what it once was.*

III

Weathering The Storm

Courage

I sometimes choose the path
that scares me the most,
because it is the path
that's going to help me grow.

The minute I decide
to conquer my doubts and fears
is the moment everything shifts
in my favour.

Someday the stars will align,
the sun will shine radiantly,
and all I have to do is follow
and bask in their light.

Imperfect

Everyone can mess up.
I can try to life-proof everything,
I will still make bad judgements,
but my true worth will never diminish.

Errors are a part of our humanity.
I hope to never run out of reasons
to stay humble and be honest about
my many imperfections.

What lies within are lessons.
Bringing out the best from the worst
in the face of missteps and struggles
is what I aim to ironically perfect.

I want imperfection to be
the very definition of me.
I will keep making mistakes, but –
it is always what I do next that counts.

Tough Times

In the pursuit of my dreams,
I unintentionally nurture
every doubt and hesitation I have.

Tried the hardest to resist,
I noticed I was pushing myself
precariously to the edge.

I began to see the dark corners
and murky junctions of what once was
a clear and direct path.

In my daunting journey,
I often lost my way.

It took a while but I realised,
It is okay to start slow.
It's okay to be down and out.
It's okay to stumble along the way.

This life,
though full of beautiful imagery and desires -
is far from perfect.

It may have taken
every motivation to keep going
but I know I am doing the best I can,
and I am capable, even on days
I thought I couldn't push through.

Growth Takes Time

I believe to render a life more meaningful;
I must be willing to go out from my snug little shell.
Adapting to change may sometimes take
days to weeks, months to years even.
If taking time meant
building confidence, self-worth, and courage,
I would welcome it like a close friend.

The truth about growth is that
it happens differently for everyone.

In certain situations, it's bizarre how a second that
ticks could feel like an eternity. Sometimes teaching
moments happen in as little as a blink of an eye.
Despite how fleeting that moment may be,
in it could hold the power to change a life forever.

No matter how hard and rough life could get,
I'm willing to stay patient,
 to be understanding of my own personal journey,
and kind to my own growth.

I may have unknowingly put myself
in places of uncertainty at times,
I know not to take any moment for granted
and use them to make things brighter and better.

Venturing beyond my comfort zone might be
daunting, but I know it will be rewarding.
It will be so significant that I wouldn't rue
freeing myself from my own constraints to
discover my life's calling.

Sailing

I love my life.
I am confident that I will always be stronger than
the problems attempting to bring me down.
So many instances in my life have
been bizarre yet just as memorable.

In the back of my mind,
I feel the price of my happiness will cost me
something terrible, which is why I'm afraid
to unfurl my sails and set out to sea.

Through my travels through life,
I've learnt that bad days always come
but just like any other day,
it too will have its dusk and dawn.

Silence could sometimes be tormenting
but it also taught me to listen
to the sound of I make deep within.
In the deafening stillness,
there I find peace.

Hard days also have their hours and minutes.
In those tiniest moments, I find reasons to carry on.
I hardened my heart and mind enough
so I never surrender during the toughest of times
 and find little pockets of clarity to see myself through.

I have drowned in my own puddles of tears before,
so much that I have now learned
to stay afloat in deep waters.
I now watch myself turn from a tiny boat
into a vessel capable of braving the strongest tides.

Just as it Should

I may never find a reason to stop moving,
even if life veers me from the path I set out to follow.
I may never see a reason to stop believing,
even if giving up is all there is for me to do.

I am able to face life bravely
and resist letting other people's opinion of me
drag me down.

I hope I can empathise with what others are going through,
even when no words are spoken,
even my actions aren't quite strong enough.
I wish to learn how to put away
my fears of being dejected, and instead,
support others' healing in ways that are right to them.

Life is a labyrinth.
The only way to get out of it is to keep moving.
I have learned that it's okay to get lost once in a while.
I use these instances to pause, rest, and refocus.

Eventually,
amidst life's haste and confusion,
I always manage to find my way through.

New You

It's slowly getting better.

I don't know when or how it started,
but I feel better than I used to.
Maybe this is what happens when I take my time
and learn to just let go of things beyond my control.

I woke up one day and felt lighter.

The baggage I carried within me disappeared.
The pain and hatred I once had
were no longer present in my heart
and grief was no longer taking much
of my thoughts.

I bid goodbye to my inhibitions,
and the things that used to mean everything to me
were no longer lighting a fuse under me.

I have discovered a different facet of life.
It did take time to mend myself,
but it happened at a pace I could keep up with.

I patiently waited.
I stayed.
I became better.

Finally

Finally –

Anger is no longer here.
My grudges seemed to have melted away.
Sadness ceased to visit.
And now, I am allowing myself to move on
and heal from the affliction of a painful past.

Finally –

I am opening new windows of opportunity
with a fresh set of perspectives.
This time, I am learning to view things clearly
without harbouring bitterness.
I've become adept at tracing the cycle of pain
that I could see where it starts,
and where it should end.

Finally –

I am mastering the art of dancing in the rain,
during the downpour of possibilities.

Finally –

I am freed from the prison I forced myself to live in;
I am getting out of the confines of self-blame
and the thought of not being good enough.
I am learning to see things differently.
Now I feel more at ease with
myself and comfortable with where I am at.

respect   self-care

love   kindness

acceptance   forgiveness

inner peace   healing

Finally –

It has become clear to me that not
everything can be perfect the first time around.
In the end, I have realised the only person
who can completely stay with me
is the person I see in the mirror every day.

Finally –

I've learned to take things gently as they come.
I've learned to love myself
a little more as time passes by.

Change

Change is necessary,
but it's a bit of a process to figure out.

Questions like
what to do,
where to go,
and how to get through it -
linger day to night.

But perhaps this is where it all starts.
It starts with questioning
where I want to see my future self.

Until I have the answers,
I will write down every question
I have about what tomorrow may bring
and the visions of a future I want to see.

Perhaps this will ignite the spark I once had,
like a curious soul wondering whether or not
there is something magical beyond
the world I know.

Like the starry-eyed wanderer I was
in my younger years,
I wish to be just curious enough
to realise that change can be a beautiful thing.

Away and Healing

It's perfectly alright to take a step back,
to be inaccessible.
There is no shame in being a short-lived character
when people expect you to stay for a long time.
You are entitled to come and go,
just like everybody else –
and that's okay.

Sometimes, moving away brings healing.
As you distance yourself from the madness of reality,
perhaps you will be able to remedy your troubled mind.
May you have the opportunity
to calm your damaging thoughts and belt out
all the screams in your heart.

I hope, one day, you will no longer feel guilty
for putting yourself first. Never be scared of
attempting to rebuild yourself again, and
never be afraid to do so alone.

Be Kind to Yourself

Life is not a race.
In this tumultuous world we're in,
I hope you find a safe corner
to be still with your thoughts.
I hope you take every chance to rest and recuperate.

The world may be evolving so fast that
you lose sight of your own progress.
Amid the riotous beauty enveloping you,
sometimes you may feel left behind.

I hope you give yourself permission to just be,
untethered from the shackles of society's beliefs.
Despite what everyone is going through,
life, as you know it, will continue to go on.

Life will always follow the endless trail
it embarked upon.
It will not turn its back for you.
It will not remind you of its swiftness or its delay.

I hope you treat yourself with kindness
in every shape and form,
each new day that dawns.

IV

Better Days

Getting By

My poems don't always rhyme.
My words aren't always on point.
My songs aren't always on the right track.
My dreams aren't always hitting home.

There are a thousand moments
when I feel lost and confused –
moments in my life when I have
thousands of questions to ask,
when I have only needed one answer.

Sometimes,
I appear as a stark reality to some
and a nostalgic memory to others.
I may not perceive myself as well as others do,
but I believe, someday,
the melancholy within my heart will gradually fade,
allowing me to see the true beauty
that lies beyond the haze.

Despite the lingering, unfamiliar echoes
that resonate louder than a heartbeat,
I find joy even in my most smallest of triumphs.

I am glad I made it this far.
I am glad I didn't stop.
I am glad I still want to go further.
Because when I had the chance to give up—
when the world already expected me to lose—

I did not.

Beauty in the Waiting

Find solace in the thought
that there is always beauty in the waiting.

Like how a rainbow slowly adorns the sky
after ceaseless rain.

It becomes a beautiful sight to behold,
and only then,
does the waiting makes sense.

Just as how life should be.

Self-Love

Find a moment,
a precious pocket of time,
amidst the demands of this busy world,
to extend a hand of care to the person
who needs it most -

yourself.

In the whirlwind of responsibilities and the
constant pull of obligations, take a pause,
even a short one -

to breathe in the soothing air of self-compassion.

Find solace in a quiet moment,
a warm cup of tea, a stroll in nature,
or the pages of a beloved book.

May you listen to your own needs,
acknowledge your own dreams,
and follow the path unique to your heart.

Heartfelt Confessions

In the comforting silence of night,
I find myself in a world gently transformed,
blanketed by a serene stillness.
It is as if the universe has thoughtfully dimmed the lights,
inviting me to indulge in quiet contemplation.

It's as if the night, with its array of stars,
beckons me to a place where my thoughts can wander,
unburdened by the hustle and bustle of each day.
It's a time when doubts come beneath me,
when dreams begin to take shape,
and the secrets I've never spoken aloud are being heard.

I am grateful for moments when it feels like
I'm sharing heartfelt confessions with the universe.

Here,
my heart finds solace,
my fears are accepted,
and the pain of reality fades,
allowing the promise of a beautiful tomorrow
be fulfilled.

Different

I'm free to be different.
I'm allowed to forge my own path,
whether I choose the one familiar to me
or the one less travelled.

And when I find myself at a crossroads,
I know I'm allowed to turn left or right, to walk or run.
It's okay to move at my own pace toward my goal,
and it doesn't matter if I go fast or slow.

I'm free to be different,
from how I like my coffee
to the many emotions I'm able to feel.
I'm allowed to indulge in my feelings,
whether I want to reflect alone when I'm sad
or be with somebody because I need to vent.

It's okay to be who I am.
I'm allowed to dance like crazy, to sing my heart out,
to scribble a poem, and be my own artist.
I know I have the power to create beautiful things.

Society is free to view me differently.
They could be judgemental of me or hold me favourably,
but ultimately, their opinion doesn't define me.
As long as I know that I live as my own definition of me,
what I think of me, is all that matters.

Just like how flowers bloom with many dazzling colours,
how trees grow at varying heights,
the rivers flow however and to wherever,
all of them are their own definitions of beauty.

I hope I can live my life as colourful as the rainbow.
I want to feel free showering the world with different colours,
and whatever shade I feel like throwing in,
I know that it's still going to be lovely,
and there is always someone out there who understands
and appreciates how multi-coloured or different I want to be.

Healing

I'm still in the process of healing
from the things I never talk about,
with scars below the surface
left by betrayal, failure, and rejection.
But I cling to the hope of finding peace and victory
after all my silent battles.

I've learned never to doubt the power of prayer,
understanding that someone hears me,
even in the quietest moments when words fail.
My faith remains unwavering,
a steady belief in the promise of better days.

Just like leaves that grow from once-bare trees
or the flowers that bloom after long winter months,
just like the courageous rainbow that emerges
after a forceful storm—

soon, I too, will be okay.

I'll grow stronger.
I'll discover my own path to healing.

This Love

Love dances on hardwood floors
in the middle of the night.
In the warped silence,
its perfection takes centre stage.
All we've known converges here,
every comfort and struggle,
with courage, we engage.

A love bestowed by the universe,
radiant and bright,
A love I dare not let slip from my sight,
It cradles me like a tender, unwavering night,
As celestial passions conspire to alight.

This, and even more –

The love I yearn to inscribe.

Alone and Complete

This is the vision I hold for myself
on an ordinary day –

a vision of simplicity, serenity, and inner peace.

Solitary moments have consistently been my sanctuary,
providing me respite from the demands of everyday life.

This is a reminder that I can find joy, peace,
and completeness within myself.

It's here that I truly see and embrace the person I am,
unburdened by the expectations of world outside.

So, this is how I aspire to welcome the
coming days ahead –

with an unwavering commitment to simplicity,
a serene heart,
and with a profound sense of peace
that comes from knowing that I am complete
in my solitude.

A Shared Journey

When life's burdens press upon me,
there's a comforting truth I hold dear –
that I'm not going through it alone.

Out there,
I realise that there are countless others
holding onto dreams,
facing their fears,
and hanging to hopes,
much like I am.

It's a heart-warming feeling that
many have walked this very path before me.

I somehow gather the strength to rise above,
no matter how painful it seems.
I persevere, no matter how slim
the chance of success is because I understand
that we are all part of this shared process —

a journey where rejections,
triumphs, tears, and laughter,
weave themselves into our lives,
binding yours with mine.

Healed and Happy

I awaken to a brand-new day,
free from pain and the burdens of my past.
My legs no longer tremble as I embark on new adventures,
and the world seems clearer,
radiant with optimism shining before my eyes.

I effortlessly trek daunting terrain and perilous waters.
New adventures are welcomed with open arms,
unburdened by the fear of disappointment.
Contentment settles within me,
like an old friend who never really left my side.

My sense of pride has been redefined,
and anger has finally subsided.
Suffering is a thing of the past;
my true worth now shines brightly for all to see.

Slowly but surely,
I'm learning to appreciate life,
despite not knowing if it will ever meet my expectations.
My former joyful self is beginning to resurface,
and my scars are fading, gradually disappearing.

I suddenly realize that darker days are behind me.
Now, I can smell the fresh fragrance of hopefulness
as I discover the good in goodbye.
It's been quite a long time,
u but I'm glad I chose to move forward.

I hope I realise that I deserve every bit of this happiness,
just as I was supposed to have it even back then.

I Can't to I Can

There are so many "*I can'ts*" in this world
that stem from anxiety and self-doubts.

It's high time I stopped giving too much value
to what the world expects of me.
Society may have its opinions and
subtly try to dictate what I should do,
but I've come to realise that none of it truly matters.

I'm giving myself permission to pursue
what I genuinely believe is best for me.
I want it to be normal to tune out the noise
of peoples' expectations and do
what's best for me.

This time around,
I'm encouraging myself to climb those fences
that I've built up over the years and
explore the world that lies beyond them.
I want to see just how far I can go
by pushing through the barriers I've created.

Sometimes, the only way to make progress
is to diverge from the old bridges I used to take
that is no longer on my path.
With courage, I'm ready to move forward
and not look back until it's time to do so.

Letting it Be

I've travelled down many winding and challenging roads,
often feeling lost and disoriented.
These travels have been my teachers,
revealing the depths of my capabilities.

There are moments I need to remind myself
how I've managed to navigate the uncharted curves
and downhill stretches on this path.
Yet looking back in those moments,
all I can see are dark and covered trails.

I may be far from perfect, but I've grown.
I may not have all the knowledge in the world,
but I've remained open to learning.
I've learned to bend without breaking,
embracing boldness,
and giving myself the grace and recognition.

I've allowed the world to take me in its revolutions,
letting time flow while moments unfold.
No one can tell if I have made an impact on this life,
but I became the way I am
because I let the world make its mark on me.

V

Keep Going

Not Giving Up

I get frustrated every time I feel like
I've done everything right, and yet, things still go wrong.
No matter how hard I try or how much effort I put in,
I still fail, one way or another.

In those moments
when I lose interest in everything,
I offer myself a gentle reminder –

To persist even when the journey grows arduous.
To press on even with overbearing weight in my footsteps.
To forge a path ahead, even if it means
treading an unknown road.
To keep believing, even in the face of insurmountable odds.

I rest, by all means, when weariness sets in,
for I know, I need strength to complete my journey.

Every step, even the hard ones,
bears witness to my resilience.
In the face of adversity, I must not give up;
instead,
I shall live with hope and continue on.

What's Next

While it has been a good and comfortable life
that I have been living, I still feel incomplete.
I never realised how draining it can be
to embrace the everyday and
be content with what I've been given.

I've had the privilege of exploring my passions,
acknowledging my limitations,
and broadening my boundaries,
yet my heart continues to yearn for more.

I know I have more skills to refine,
blank pages of my everyday life
to fill with words or scrap entirely,
but I will keep writing because I know
I can add more definitions to my story.

I know I still have piles of doubt hidden in locked chests
and more battles with myself I hope to best
Nevertheless, I will keep going because I know I can.

So here's to the troubled past
I am about to leave behind,
to the remnants of my misery
I should stop trying to revive.

I am leaving behind
the scars and wounds from my failed efforts,
the echoes of my unheard wishes,
and every explanation I thought I needed.

Instead of dreading what was
and what was supposed to be,
I will be taking in the worthwhile experiences,
the insights, and the irreplaceable memories
from this obstacle-strewn journey.

I don't know what awaits me,
but I will be taking the best parts of me
into the next chapter.

Better You

It's quite tedious how sometimes
I would argue with myself,
yet there are moments when my heart just wavers,
my emotions take over.

I know not if all my decisions are right
but with the good I keep in my heart,
I am confident that I am able to find peace
in the choices I make.

Right now, I am building resilience
so I can stay strong despite the pressures,
breathe easy amidst the chaos,
and keep calm when everything seems overwhelming.

Sometimes being graceful in the thick of adversity
doesn't always end favourably, but –

I am learning to love and support myself more.

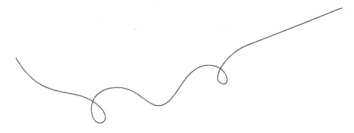

Looking back to who I was years ago,
I never would have thought I'd become
who I am today when dealing with uncertainty.

Despite constantly getting lost in my travels
through life, I could always rely on
the faith and trustI have put in myself
and find wherever it is my soul feels at peace
and where I believe it will get the love it deserves.

Cruel Universe

I no longer seek to appease the universe...
or beg for gentleness from its heavy hands.

I will allow it to hurt me if it must.
I will allow it to give me trials
however daunting they may be.
I will allow it to lead me to the wrong people
or introduce whichever uncertainty
it chooses to give me.

I will live through whatever calamity
it may smite upon me.
I will no longer expect the universe to
shower me with love or kindness.
I will allow it to tear me up or knock me down.

No matter how loud I scream,
or no matter how far away I run,
the whims of the universe will remain absolute,
 but I'll keep living.

I will keep going.

The universe may give me
a thousand battles to fight,
it may even give me
more reasons to give up,
but I will let these turn me
into someone they can't easily break.

I will proudly wear every cut and scar
like bright stars shining in a moonless sky
and it will be my armour as I navigate life
and live it however I choose.

Making it Through

I always manage to find hope and faith
deep within myself, like a comforting embrace
for my wounded soul.

Life has its way of surprising me with its beauty,
allowing me to rise above the ashes
of my painful experiences.

I've pulled through the toughest of times,
even when it felt like I was walking on a tightrope,
hoping not to fall.

I've shown resilience during my darkest hours.

Tomorrow may hide its secrets,
but it holds the promise of new adventures
and beautiful tales yet to be written.
Although the path ahead may seem formidable,
I find comfort in the firmness of my choices,
my unconditional love for life,
and the endless spools I have to weave
to make dreams a reality.

I'm here to grow and embrace life's journey,
knowing that I can overcome anything.

I believe I can do more.
I can be more.

What's Beyond

I always view what's yet to come with optimism.
What has always been there for me,
filling the light in my eyes and weightlessness
in my steps, is HOPE.

Hope is the warmth that greets me in the morning,
making the coldness of what once was,
be a distant memory.

I believe my journey is far from its conclusion.
The stops along the way might feel desolate at times,
but it's okay.

I guess, a part of one's growth is
learning the good that comes from leaving.
I've now found succour in chasing the unknown.
I'm embracing every opportunity that comes my way.

And maybe, just maybe –
I have outgrown my fears.

And maybe, just maybe –
this is me telling the world,
I am more than ready to face what more it has in store.

With a faint glow always on the horizon,
I no longer feel alone in my struggles.
I am no longer hesitant to take one step after another
for I know forward is the only way that matters.

Together

So much happened over the years
Look how far we've come, we're still here
I always knew your love
was the only constant thing
Having you near me, I've got nothing to fear

I give you all my days and countless nights
We've slowed dance our love
through songs as lovers might
Go to beaches, falls, and mountains,
and see the world in all its heights

Please know
you are the one thing I have done right

You are always next to me
as I fill in these empty pages
Every letter to words,
every line budding into a prose

With new adventures to try
or another dream to chase
I wish to be with you
as I go through each phase

From morning walks and coffees
down to evening kisses –
This is our promise to pursue
This is the beautiful life I dream of,
together with you.

Proud of Me

People say there's something waiting for us out there,
so I'm determined to seize my opportunities and
witness life's breathtaking panoramas.

'Tis only when I ventured that I realised
beautiful things are given to those
who dare to strive and pursue,
even when in fear's clutches.

When a door closes,
searching for and opening new ones is up to me
as life does not stop to console me
for my regrets and missed opportunities.

I discovered that while life is a gruelling expedition,
it's transformative.
At its best, it inspires me to believe in my ability
to go leaps and bounds, even when I thought
I never had it in me.

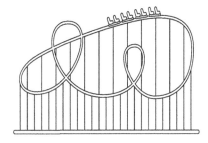

On the perplexing and demanding days,
my travels have taught me to take the leap
when I am at the top and land whenever I fall.
They have shown me how to find life's lessons
in every moment.

I would never have gotten here if I had
stopped believing that I could.
Despite my fears, I have forged
and will keep forging ahead,
and for that –

I am proud of myself.

You are Beautiful

I hope you capture snapshots
in the form of memories for every beautiful
moment you share with yourself.

Appreciate your voice for speaking the truth.
Be grateful for your dreams for giving you hope,
and your ambitions for giving you strength to
pursue your passions.
Admire your hands, as they create so much;
respect your body for being capable,
and your heart for being fearless.

May you embrace all the quirks and craziness
within you, and tell them -

they're beautiful too.

Life's Seasons

I came to the realisation that life is not a perpetual spring,
an unending cascade of joy and gratitude.
Sometimes, it involves pain and sorrow,
or acts of letting go of old, dull memories
to create new beginnings.

The changing of the season is all about
recognising that life has no predefined limits.
Often, we tend to forget that the most challenging
situations that come in the shortest of moments
offer lessons that endure a lifetime.

I hope, whether the skies are grey
or there's not a cloud in sight,
we continue to embrace change
just as much change has settled into our lives.

May we grow through each kind of weather,
in every season, for reasons that matter most.

Exceptional

Embrace your uniqueness, your individuality,
even the parts of yourself
you may not always find lovely.

Show the shades they don't want to see.
Speak the things everyone is afraid to say,
be your own personal advocate.

Paint a portrait of you
where your image exudes boldness
and confidence.

Unbind yourself from the strings
society tied on you, in hopes of getting you move
the way they want you to.

Be unapologetically you,
even if the rest of the world fails to agree.
Applaud who you are –

an imperfect person, capable of perfection.

Celebrate your silly quirks, your unique skills,
and all there is that only you find meaningful.
Celebrate all your little milestones
and your tiny bits of progress.
Embrace all the mistakes you've made
in your attempts at learning.

Be confident and own your flaws.
Be a beacon that's radiant in your own colours
in a world where everyone else is content
with blending in.

Staying on Track

I will not be bound by my doubts and hesitations.
Sometimes all it takes is getting
out of bed, opening the window,
taking in the fresh scent of dawn,
and telling myself that today is a new day
where I can try again.

I want to nourish myself
with all good things surrounding me
until my heart and mind begin to feel
I can accomplish anything I aspire to.

I'm going to allow myself to wander, without fear.
I will do a short stroll through the park
or do a bicycle trip through the countryside.
Whatever I choose to do,
I can form beautiful connections,
I'd find new routines and discover fresh passions
to complement old ones.

Sometimes taking a detour doesn't mean
I no longer wish to arrive at my destination.
A shift of scenery or a change of pace can often be
what I need to take me where I need to be.

I know not when I'll get to where I want to go
or, whether or not I even get there.
It might even be that my dreams get realised
by the ones I hold dear
and the view I wished to see will be from their eyes.

Even then –

The course I set out on
have always been for the realisation of my dreams.

Tales of Bravery

I'm going to give myself
the chance to seek what is out there.
I want to be someone who's going to welcome
the world with less expectation and more positivity.

Just like sailing without setting a course,
I'm going to push myself to venture to a new coast,
to someplace where different novelties
are waiting for me.

I want to be someone who wants
to keep soaring to new heights.
Like how birds are without a care
about the mayhem that's beneath them,
I am going to go where my wings carry me.

I will stop searching for the easiest roads
and most convenient shortcuts.
I will give myself the opportunity to experience
the world in its most natural conditions.

I will turn my failures and rejections into
plotlines that bring more meaning to my story.
For certain, there will be chapters worth reading
and some parts I wish I had never known.

I will allow myself to fall, so that rising up
would bring me a greater sense of accomplishment,
and so that every dark chapter that comes next
will only fill me with hope and optimism.

And this is the portrait of the world I want to paint,
the tales of bravery I want to write.

Taking Risks

Let this be my story of success.
I want to be the one who isn't afraid
to see the world for what it is,
the one who isn't afraid to take a leap of faith
and go after opportunities for a more beautiful,
happier life.

Let this be my history –
one that will chronicle my growth
and tales of valour.

I hope I find the courage to trust life again
after every time it gets me down.
I hope I continue to believe in myself
and how I am capable of amazing things.

I'll forgive myself if I fail to understand things.
Sometimes, it does matter how hard I try.

Doing often starts from trying.

Like a Sunflower

Life unfolds as a series of tiny steps.
Like how a flower comes to bloom to meet the sun,
the earth gives us life so we could start
budding and blossoming.

I wish to have a phase
where I can brim gloriously vividly.
I may not be at that point just yet,
but until then I will shower in light.

During my time on this earth,
I know I will go through phases
and weather storms I cannot avoid.
I will never bend or break as long as I can choose to grow.

Even the frailest tree welcomes a ray of sunlight
peeking through the clouds after a downpour.

I too will have moments that will make me
stand firm when I'm about to crumble
and will keep me believing when I'm on the brink
of losing hope.
I will be entangled in life's twists and turns,
but I'll learn to find my way and rise above it all.

I may not always realise it but simply waking up each day,
breathing in the morning air, and starting everyday anew
is a reminder that life continues to unfold
in countless unique ways.

With it comes the gentle push that keeps me moving forward,
even when the many paths I take seem uncertain.

In the midst of the darkest days,
I wish to be like a sunflower.
It never stops *searching for light*
even in its most *difficult moments.*

Just as it stands unwavering,
weathering the storms that come its way
I, too, will have
better and sunshiny days.

With determination,
I will endeavour to *keep going,*
embracing the hopeful light
that awaits beyond the shadows.

Made in United States
North Haven, CT
11 May 2024

52388440R10093